Dresden
FLOWER GARDEN

A NEW TWIST ON TWO QUILT CLASSICS

Blanche Young and
Lynette Young Bingham

C&T PUBLISHING

© 2003, Blanche Young and Lynette Young Bingham

Editor-in-Chief: Darra Williamson

Editor and Technical Editor: Ellen Pahl

Copyeditor/Proofreader: Gael Betts / Susan Nelsen

Cover Designer: Kristen Yenche

Design Director/Book Designer: Kristen Yenche

Illustrator: Richard Sheppard

Production Assistants: Timothy Manibusan and Lucas Mulks

Quilt Photography: Sharon Risedorph, except as noted

How-to Photography: Diane Pedersen and Lynn Koolish

Published by C&T Publishing, Inc., P.O. Box 1456, Lafayette, California 94549

Front Cover Image: *Rhapsody in Blue*, Blanche Young

Back Cover Images: *In My Thirties Garden*, Lynette Young Bingham

Stock Photography used throughout the book courtesy of Photospin.com

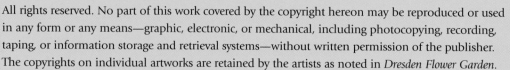

Library of Congress Cataloging-in-Publication Data

Young, Blanche.

Dresden flower garden : a new twist on two quilt classics / Blanche Young and Lynette Young Bingham.

p. cm.

Includes index.

ISBN 1-57120-192-0

1. Patchwork--Patterns. 2. Quilting--Patterns. I. Bingham, Lynette Young, II. Title.

TT835 .D72 2003

746.46'041--dc21

2002011910

Printed in USA

10 9 8 7 6 5 4 3 2 1

Contents

Dedication

This book is dedicated to the memory of Blanche's mother and Lynette's grandmother, Elnora Mattie Day Stringfellow Boberg (1883-1966). Mattie was born and lived her entire life in the small town of Draper, Utah, located at the southernmost end of the Salt Lake Valley. Mattie was a master gardener and known for her beautiful flower gardens. Her passion for color and beauty was her legacy to her family. May this link to our past be always remembered, treasured, and shared with future generations.

Acknowledgments

What a pleasure it has been to work with the professional and friendly staff of C&T Publishing, most notably Lynn Koolish, Darra Williamson, Kristen Yenche, and Diane Pedersen—we thank you. We also give our heartfelt thanks to our editor, Ellen Pahl, for her expertise and knowledge. It has been a unique, long-distance relationship, with us in Utah and Ellen in Pennsylvania, so we are also thankful for e-mail!

In the process of having eight of the quilts machine quilted for this book, we have found a new friend in Marian Gallian. With little direction from us, she used her talents to make the quilts look fabulous. We also thank Dorothy Barnett for quilting the cover quilt, and Carol DeFelice for sharing her quilt with us.

The love, support, and encouragement received from our family have been invaluable, and they are much appreciated.

Introduction

In *Dresden Flower Garden*, we will take you on a new quilting adventure. Be prepared for something fun and relaxing, like meandering through a meadow; you can have fun using up your fabrics and stitch a quilt that resembles a bouquet of wildflowers at the same time. This wonderful new design combines two traditional and nostalgic favorites, Grandmother's Flower Garden and Dresden Plate, to create an original, new treasure.

This book covers all aspects of making these unique, colorful quilts—from design, color and fabric selection, to the rotary cutting, easy piecing, and simple appliqué needed to create them. You don't have to worry about handpiecing hexagons or doing a lot of hand appliqué. We provide instructions for several quilts, with an alternate size for each. There's sure to be at least one that is perfect for you! If not, follow your imagination and our directions to fashion your own variation. There are several setting options and unlimited border possibilities, resulting in almost infinite number of innovative quilts that you can make.

In addition to instructions for making the four quilts, we've included additional quilts to inspire you and serve as testimony to the endless variations possible with this fun block.

All of Blanche's previous books have dealt with very exacting color placements of light and dark fabrics. *Dresden Flower Garden* has been a delightful and liberating escape—to design and make a quilt where there are no rules! Well, there is just one small rule; you'll read about that in Chapter 2, "Fabric, Color, and Value." It's an easy one to follow, or not, as you prefer!

Blanche Young is very excited to introduce her latest quilt design to quilters, as well as Lynette Young Bingham, her newest co-author. Lynette is the third of Blanche's four daughters to work with her on a subject that she holds almost as near and dear to her heart as her daughters—Quilts!

Now, look through the book, and take a stroll through a *Dresden Flower Garden*. You'll find plenty of ideas and inspiration plus all the help you'll need to create a wildflower bouquet of your own.

Blanche and Lynette

The Path to Dresden Flower Garden

Blanche is known throughout the world of quilting as having the ability to take a traditional design and create new, efficient methods of construction. If her career had not taken her into quilting, she probably would have been an engineer! She has the uncanny ability and vision to analyze a pattern, alter the design, and create a new spin-off using timesaving techniques and shortcuts. She's a whirlwind in the sewing room!

In her travels and through teaching, she has had many opportunities to study both old and new quilt designs. The inspiration for this particular design came about in 1995 when Blanche was looking at photographs of two similar quilt designs, the Wagon Wheel and the Endless Chain. She became fascinated with the two designs, but did not like the alternating light and dark sections within each block. She felt it created a choppy look.

Wagon Wheel and Endless Chain are similar designs that contain pieced hexagons of alternating light and dark sections. They connect at the dark sections, creating an interlocking design. Both designs are created by piecing together twelve patches to form a hexagon.

Endless Chain or Wagon Wheel

Blanche was able to see a connection between the pieced hexagon in both Wagon Wheel and Endless Chain, and the Dresden Plate block. The typical Dresden Plate, a favorite of quilters throughout the 1930s and 1940s, is a basic hexagon shape made up of twelve sections; each piece has a pointed or scalloped edge. By taking the point off every other section, a hexagon is created. The Dresden Plate pattern is traditionally a pieced and appliquéd block.

Dresden Plate

Once Blanche saw the hexagonal shape of the Dresden Plate, she related that look with the familiar Grandmother's Flower Garden pattern. This design is created by sewing together many small hexagons, usually six hexagons surrounding a seventh, creating a rosette or flower. Many wonderful quilts were made using this extremely popular pattern of six-sided shapes; usually the pieced "flower" units were then pieced with other solid-colored hexagons to create the "path" through Grandmother's Flower Garden.

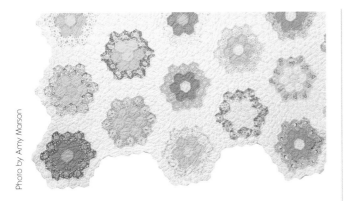

Grandmother's Flower Garden

Blanche realized that if she constructed twelve-section hexagons—reminiscent of the Dresden Plate pattern—and sewed them up against each other, it would create a design similar to an enlarged version of the Grandmother's Flower Garden. Hence the name: Dresden Flower Garden.

Where It All Began 1995

76" x 96"

Large blocks, pieced and machine quilted by Blanche Young.

Blanche took it one step further. She wanted the pieced hexagons to be sewn next to each other, creating a solid field of blossoms! She originally envisioned making the quilt with each block or "plate" in red fabrics. Each red block gradated from light to dark red as the colors went around within each block. She made up many red blocks and began to sew them together–and hated it! She realized that she needed to add other colors. She then made blocks with other colors, some with varying values from light to dark, and others with the value of each color similar within each plate. Her original quilt *Where It All Began* is shown below.

Blanche specifically did not want to "plan" the placement of the blocks in her quilts. She did not want or like all the light blocks in the center with the darker ones around the outside, for example. The lively look and feel of this quilt and the others shown in this book are the result of randomly and spontaneously dispersing the colors in a more haphazard, unplanned, and fun fashion.

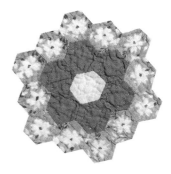

While the design certainly lends itself to a more regulated approach as well, our preference is for a free-wheeling attitude without specific arrangements of light blocks and dark blocks to give that wildflower bouquet look. Read on for more guidance on color and value choices, but feel free to interpret this design in any way you want. Follow your own path, wherever it leads you!

Fabric, Color, and Value

When you look at the quilts throughout this book, the first thing that strikes you about them is the mix of vivid colors and texture, as in a bouquet of wildflowers. The appeal of a wildflower bouquet is in its freeform blending of colors, shapes, textures, and values. Just like picking wildflowers and informally arranging them, our approach to color is rather intuitive, not strictly based on a color wheel or formal color theory.

Blanche's father, Lynette's grandfather, was a wallpaper hanger and painter. As a very young child, Blanche watched him mix colors; he would stir, add pigment, and explain what the results would be.

Lynette's grandmother, Blanche's mother, was an avid gardener. From her Blanche learned how the careful arrangement of colors in a large flower garden would enhance each other. Purple iris was always behind the yellow tulips. The peonies with their large pink, red, and white blossoms would be near the purple larkspurs or the early lavender phlox. Orange and yellow marigolds always sported a border of purple ageratum and blue lobelia. While she may not have used the term *complementary colors,* that's exactly how she gardened. Blanche absorbed color knowledge from both parents. Color was always an important aspect of her life, and it still is.

The making of these quilts can be a liberating experience, allowing you to just have fun with your fabrics. While there is that element of freedom, there are also some general guidelines regarding color and fabric choices that will help you make the most successful quilt. You don't need to learn all about color theory, but it's important to understand what we mean by color families and value.

Color and Value

The color "families" are the primary and secondary colors on the color wheel: red, orange, yellow, green, blue, and violet. In making your Dresden Flower Garden, you have the opportunity to use many different fabrics. Make sure you have a wide variety of fabrics in each color and also a good variety of fabrics of similar value within each color family.

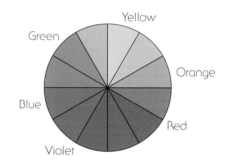

Color wheel families

Value is the lightness or darkness of a color. All colors come in many values, from lightest lights (pastels), to mediums, and to the very dark. It is the use of value, rather than color, that is most critical to bringing out the charming character and stunning visual effects that are possible with this quilt design. You can have gorgeous fabrics and fabulous colors, but if the values are not harmonious, your quilt will not be either.

Generally, these quilts are most successful when each block is made from fabrics of similar value, or fabrics that blend with each other. That allows the block to be perceived as a cohesive hexagonal shape, rather than an assemblage of twelve assorted patches. The values may change from block to block, as well as color, but this is really the only "rule" that we follow when making the blocks and quilts.

Choosing both a variety of colors and values to create your quilt results in endless possibilities: all light fabrics, a mixture of light and dark, or medium and dark. Make all the blocks in one color family for a lovely monochromatic look; make each block a different color to create the variegated, wildflower bouquet look. The blocks below illustrate the use of one value in each block.

We find that blocks made of a wide variety of fabrics make the quilt more interesting. Blanche loves to use florals and bright bold fabrics, since that is what she tends to collect. Use whatever you have on hand; just keep the idea of value in mind when arranging the patches for each block. No one patch should stand out noticeably from the others.

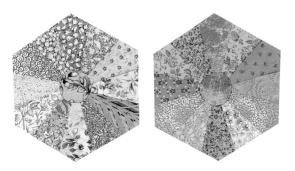

Blocks made of light value fabrics

Blocks made from all floral fabrics

Blocks made of medium value fabrics

Block made from bold fabrics

Another option is to create gradated blocks by placing fabrics in a light to dark arrangement. The fabrics should blend from one to the next around the block, similar to a colorwash quilt.

Blocks made of dark value fabrics

Blocks made from gradated values

Fabric Selection

When it comes to choices of quilting fabrics, the sky's the limit! We are so fortunate to have an almost infinite selection of good quality 100% cotton fabrics available in quilt and fabric shops today. Always use good quality fabrics of similar weight. This makes your sewing easier and more accurate.

Quilters instinctively buy fabric that they just cannot resist, and they buy the colors they love. You can tell pretty quickly what a quilter's favorite color is by looking at her fabric stash. In Lynette's sewing room, you'll find lots of pinks, purples, greens, reproduction fabrics, novelty prints, and plaids. Blanche prefers florals of all types and bold geometric prints. Her early quilts were primarily earth tones and autumn shades, but as she has grown in her quiltmaking, she has gotten out of her color rut as she puts it!

One of the exciting things for us in making these quilts is that we have not gone out to buy new fabric. It's such a good feeling to see our stacks of fabric dwindling. (Then, later on, we can justify buying yet more fabric to fill the shelves back up!) We have, however, taken our completed, pieced blocks to the quilt shop to purchase fabric for borders, backing, and binding.

These quilts are a scrap saver's dream come true! Leftover fabrics, scraps, and extra strips from other projects are perfect. Even smaller scraps can be used for the appliquéd center circles. This is also a wonderful fat quarter project for those who can't resist buying those charming bundles. Luscious hand-dyed fabrics in gradated colors are perfect for blocks of gradated values. A large variety of fabrics in each color family will usually result in a more pleasing overall effect, with a wildflower bouquet appearance. The bottom line: the more fabrics, the better!

A Note from Blanche

You'll notice that I don't include many plaids in my quilts. That's because I don't own any! I come from a dressmaking background, and I learned to avoid plaids at an early age! But don't hesitate to use them if you love them, and don't worry about matching. Stripes are fair game, as well. Use them for faux strip-pieced blocks as in the quilt *Midnight Jewel* on page 58.

Design Possibilities

Blanche does not plan her quilts in advance; they evolve. She works with her fabric stash to create beautiful blocks. Then she decides how she will set them together. Lynette is a free spirit, as well, and begins by simply cutting and sewing. We realize that not everyone is so inclined, so we've included some helpful suggestions and guidance for those who do like to plan ahead.

SIZE

The first thing you'll want to think about is the size. How big will you want your quilt to be? See the cutting charts on page 20. This will give you an idea of how many blocks you will need. If you choose to use setting triangles for the star or diamond variation, you will need fewer blocks, and your quilt will go together faster.

COLOR

Decide if you want a planned color scheme or if you prefer the freedom of the wildflower bouquet look. You can make each block a different color, or limit the number of colors. Look at the quilts shown throughout the book to decide which approach you prefer. Photocopy one of the quilt layouts on pages 59–60 if you'd like to use colored pencils to plan colors and placement on paper before you start cutting fabric.

SETTING

Once your blocks are made, use a design wall to lay them out as instructed in Chapter 4, "Setting and Border Options." You can set them side-by-side, or use one of the variations discussed in that chapter. Look through the book to get inspiration from other quilts. You may even come up with your own unique setting.

Cutting and Piecing

Dresden Flower Garden is a hybrid design, combining the best elements of two traditional designs to create a third, updated variation. The techniques we use for cutting and piecing are also hybrid combinations of both old and new methods. We've combined the use of traditional templates with rotary cutting to make the cutting as quick, easy, and efficient as possible. The piecing is streamlined as well, based on chain piecing the patches or "petals" of the blocks.

Getting Started

For the construction of the quilts in this book, you'll need standard sewing and quilting supplies, and the specific items listed below. Fabric requirements are based on a 42"-width; however, we allow for 40" of usable fabric to account for shrinkage when washing. In the cutting instructions, strips are generally cut on the crosswise grain unless you're using scraps for cutting the block patches.

Tools & Supplies

- Rotary cutter
- Rotary cutting mat
- Rotary rulers: 6" x 12" and 6" x 24"
- Revolving cutting mat (optional)
- Acrylic Dresden Flower Garden templates or template plastic
- Permanent felt tip marker
- Pencil or other fabric marker
- Scissors for cutting template plastic
- Paper plates
- Tag board or manila file folders

SEWING & PRESSING

Use an accurate ¼" seam allowance when piecing the projects. It's a good idea to do a test seam to check that your ¼" is accurate before you begin sewing your quilt. In general, press seams toward the darker fabric unless instructed otherwise. Specific pressing instructions for the blocks and projects are included throughout the book. Press lightly in an up-and-down motion. Avoid using a very hot iron or over-ironing, which can distort shapes and blocks.

CUTTING

You can make the Dresden Flower Garden blocks in three different finished sizes: small 5½", medium 8", and large 10". These are the measurements from flat side to flat side through the center. You will need templates for cutting patches for the size you choose.

TEMPLATES

You can make your own templates or purchase commercially made acrylic templates. The instructions throughout the book show the use of acrylic templates. These are handy because you can cut around them with your rotary cutter. See "Resources" on page 63 for information on purchasing these templates.

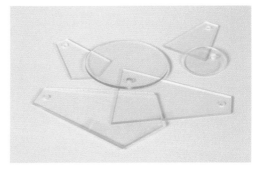

Acrylic templates for use with a rotary cutter and mat

Making Templates

To make your own templates, see the patterns for the templates on pages 61 and 62. Use either a clear or frosted template plastic; it is more durable and accurate than cardboard and makes it easier to trace the template patterns accurately. Trace the desired size Templates A and B and the larger Template C (cut size) onto the template plastic, and carefully cut out the templates along the traced lines.

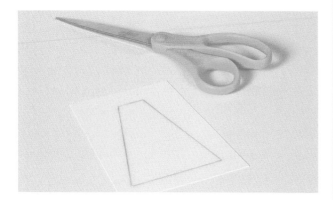

Trace the template pattern onto template plastic.

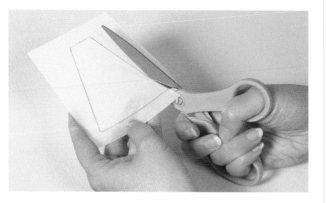

Carefully cut out the template on the drawn line.

Stabilizing Purchased Templates

If you are using purchased acrylic templates, affix small squares or circles of self-adhesive sandpaper to the "corners" and point on one side of each template. These sandpaper dots are available in quilt shops and will prevent the templates from sliding or slipping on the fabric when cutting around them.

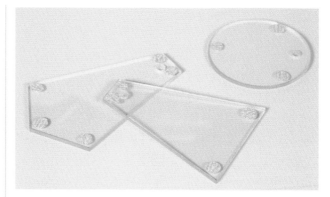

Place sandpaper dots on acrylic templates.

CUTTING STRIPS

As mentioned in the previous chapter, this is a wonderful quilt to use leftover strips and other pieces of fabric. And the best thing is that the cutting can be done on the lengthwise grain, the crosswise grain, or even on the bias! To cut patches for several blocks, we start with strips, cut using a rotary cutter.

Each block size will require a different width strip. The small 5½" blocks require strips cut 3½" wide. For the medium 8" blocks, cut strips 4½" wide, and for the large 10" blocks, cut strips 6" wide. You can use scraps, as well; it will simply require more cutting.

For the most efficient cutting, use strips that are either 21" or 42" in length. Strips cut from fat quarters will be approximately 21" long, which gives you a good strip length, plus the ability to include a wide variety of different fabrics. Remember, the most interesting and vibrant quilts feature many different fabrics. Refer to "Cutting Charts" on page 20 for specific numbers of strips to cut for various block sizes and quilt sizes.

Because the cut edges of the patches will be cut on an angle, resulting in mostly bias edges, you really don't have to worry about the fabric grain when cutting strips. In fact, you can even cut your strips at a slight angle if desired, to obtain longer lengths. If you use scraps and odd pieces of fabric, anything goes! Just arrange your template on the fabric whatever way it fits.

CUTTING THE PATCHES WITH ACRYLIC TEMPLATES

Stack and align four to eight strips of fabric, depending on how many layers you're comfortable cutting at a time. Choose strips of similar color and value. Cutting similar colors and values together will make it easier later when sorting and planning the blocks. As you cut, you need to keep the A patches separate from the B patches. Keep them in separate stacks of color families. The fabrics can be stacked either right or wrong side up; it doesn't matter.

1. Place template A on the fabric with the pointed edge away from you. Align the lower edge of the template on the cut edge of the strip. Hold the template firmly with your left hand, and use your rotary cutter to cut one of the long edges and then cut the other long edge. Separate the cut patch slightly from the strip so you can cut the angled ends without slashing into the next patch. (If you're left-handed, reverse these directions.)

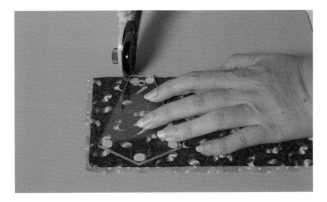

Align the lower edge of Template A with the cut edge of the strip.

2. Place template B on the fabric with the wide end toward you; align the short edge with the cut edge of the strip. Cut the long edges, separate slightly, and cut the ends to create a B patch. Continue cutting, alternating templates as shown.

Cutting diagram for the A and B patches

Remember, as you cut the patches, separate the A patches from the B patches. If space permits, keep them sorted in color families.

Keep A and B patches separate and group by color.

CUTTING WITH A REVOLVING MAT

An easy way to cut around the templates, especially when using scraps or small pieces of fabric, is to use a revolving cutting mat. There are commercially available revolving mats, such as the Brooklyn Revolver (see "Resources" on page 63), but you can also create your own by placing a small cutting mat on a flat-topped Lazy Susan.

Commercially available Brooklyn Revolver

A homemade revolving mat using a Lazy Susan with small cutting mat on top

When using a revolving mat, the cutting is fast and easy. Again, cut several layers at one time. Cut along one long edge of the template. Do not release the pressure of your hand that is holding down the template, and use your other hand (while holding your rotary cutter) to rotate the mat and cut the other long edge of the template. Rotate clockwise and continue cutting around the template in this manner until all edges have been cut.

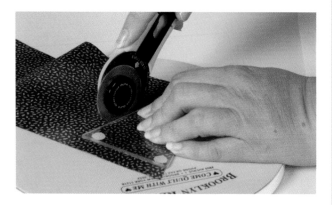

Hold the template and make a cut along the long edge of the template.

Rotate the mat and make the next cut.

Make the final cut along the last edge.

CUTTING THE PATCHES WITH PLASTIC TEMPLATES

To cut patches using plastic templates that you have made, place the templates on the wrong side of your fabric, trace around them with a sharp pencil or fabric marker. Use your rotary cutter and ruler to cut on the traced lines. You can layer your fabrics or strips as with the acrylic templates to cut more than one patch at a time. That way, you trace just once, on the top layer of fabric.

Draw around the template on the wrong side of the fabric.

Cut on the lines with a rotary cutter and ruler.

Arranging the Patches

Now comes the fun part! Once all the A and B patches are cut, you'll want to select the patches for each block. Each block requires six A patches and six B patches. Select patches for each block from fabrics of the same color and value (refer to Chapter 2).

Here's where a package of paper plates comes in handy! We discovered that they are perfect for arranging the Dresden Flower Garden blocks and keeping them organized. Use inexpensive, plain white paper plates. For the large size patches, you will need a package of 10½" plates; smaller paper plates work fine for the medium and small size patches. Lay out the twelve chosen patches on a paper plate, alternating the six A patches and six B patches around the plate.

Arrange A and B patches on a paper plate for each block.

Arranging your A and B patches this way lets you see how each block will look, and the patches are in position ready to be sewn. Many blocks can be "set up" or arranged on paper plates, and then the paper plates can be stacked. We have arranged and stacked as many as thirty to forty plates at one time. It's a great way to stay organized and keep all the small pieces together. It is easy to transport the plates to your sewing machine, and keeps the blocks orderly and in place if sewing is interrupted.

We try to avoid creating identical blocks. Although many blocks may be very similar in color, a variety of fabrics gives each block its own identity.

Sewing the Blocks

Chain piecing the blocks makes assembly quick and efficient. Piece the blocks in pairs to avoid confusion. Select two paper plates with different color blocks so you will be able to easily tell the blocks apart. Using this method, you'll complete the blocks quickly and efficiently.

1. Always begin with an A patch. It doesn't matter which A patch you begin with, but to avoid confusion, pick up the patches in a clockwise direction from your beginning point. Align the A patch right sides together with the B patch on top. Be sure that the narrow ends and the side edges are lined up with each other. Stitch with patch A on the bottom; begin sewing from the wide end of the unit to the narrow using a ¼" seam allowance. Do not cut the thread.

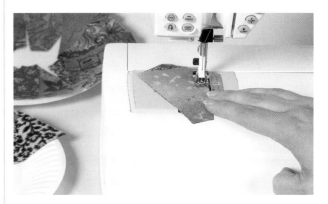

Stitch from the wide end to the narrow end.

2. Select an A patch and B patch from the second plate. Align them as you did in step 1. Butt the two patches up against the first unit and stitch. Leave the second unit in the machine.

Butt the second pair of patches against the first and sew.

3. Clip the thread between the first and second units. Bring the first unit back to the machine, open up the sewn pair, and align an A patch to the top of the B and sew. Always begin sewing at the wide ends toward the narrow ends. Select patches from the paper plate in a clockwise direction.

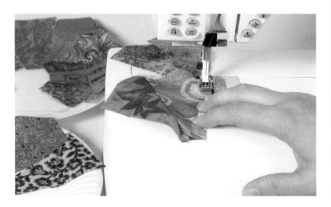

Add the third patch and chain piece the two blocks.

4. Cut the thread between the two units, and continue chain piecing in this fashion, alternating the A's and B's to complete each block. Stitch the last seam to form a "circle."

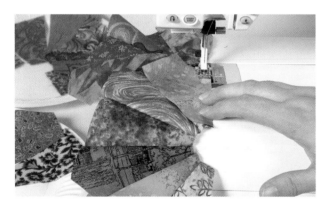

Butt each unit up against the next and sew from the wide end to the narrow.

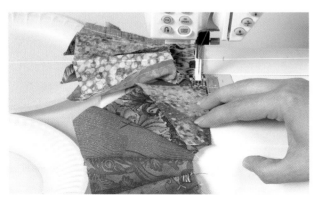

Continue adding patches until all the pieces are sewn together.

5. Place the block right side down on the ironing surface. Press the bottom half (the half closest to you) with seams going toward the left. Rotate the block and press the rest of the seams toward the left. All the seams should be pressed in a clockwise direction. Turn the block right side up and press again. It is important to make sure each seam is completely pressed and lies flat. Pressing only from the back can create small pleats at the seams.

Press on the wrong side first in a clockwise direction.

Press all the seams in the same direction.

Turn the block over and press from the right side.

The Flower Centers

The round flower centers can all be made of the same fabric (see the quilt *Cow Pies in the Sky* on page 45) or from different colors. They can contrast with the flower "petals" or blend with them. We generally make the flower centers from fabrics that blend with the A and B patches. This lets the block read as a more uniform color, or as a flower without a distinct center. The block will look more like a hexagon. Using contrasting center colors will emphasize the look of a daisy or other flower.

You can cut flower centers from squares, strips, or even the smallest scraps in your stash! You may wish to wait until you have sewn all of your blocks before deciding on the fabrics and cutting out the centers.

MAKING THE FLOWER CENTER TEMPLATES

There are two circle template patterns for each block size. The circle templates are labeled with the letter C. The larger circle is the cut size of the template, and the smaller is the finished size.

1. You will need a template for the larger circle; use the purchased acrylic template or make your own. To make a template, trace the cut-size pattern onto clear or frosted template plastic using a fine-point permanent felt marker. Cut out the template.

2. Place the larger, cut-size template on the wrong side of the flower center fabric and trace around the template using a light or dark fabric marker, depending on the color of fabric. You can stack several layers to be cut at the same time.

3. Cut the number of circles needed using fabric scissors.

⁂ *Helpful Hint from Blanche*
If you want to "fussy-cut" the centers to feature a certain design motif, color, or other floral accent, use a clear plastic template to center the motif and trace around it.

4. Make a plastic template of the smaller finished size circle, and trace it onto cardstock or other heavy paper. Cut out the circle on the drawn line.

We use old file folders for the smaller, finished size circle. The weight and density of the paper is perfect for this use. The cardstock circle can be re-used many times and will last quite a while. One will usually last for the making of a quilt, but you may want to make an extra just to have on hand. You can also use a product called Templar for the finished-size circle. It is a plastic material that can withstand ironing without melting. It is available at quilt shops and through mail-order catalogs.

PREPARING THE CENTER CIRCLES FOR APPLIQUÉ

This method of preparing and pressing the flower centers insures a perfect circle for the center each time. It also makes any type of appliqué quick and easy.

1. To prepare the centers for appliqué, stitch around each circle with a long machine basting stitch or by hand, ⅛" from the edge.

Machine baste around the cut-size circle.

2. Place the fabric flower center right side down and place the cardboard circle template in the center of the fabric circle. Gently pull the thread ends to gather the fabric around the cardboard circle.

Gather the fabric around the cardboard circle.

3. With a hot iron on the steam setting, press both sides of the circle. Use a shot of spray starch when pressing, if desired. Allow to cool. Remove the cardboard, and repeat for the rest of the centers.

Press the flower center on the cardboard template.

4. To center the circle on the block, place the center circle onto the right side of the block, with the right side of the flower center facing up. Pin in place by inserting three or four pins through the circle, as close to the outside edge as possible. Turn the block over and look at the pins to see if the circle is centered. If the pins are not evenly spaced around the opening, reposition the flower center. Pin again and check placement by viewing from the wrong side.

Place pins on the right side.

Appliquéing the Center

There are three methods of attaching the center circles to the blocks: hand appliqué, invisible machine appliqué, or machine appliqué with a decorative stitch. Choose whichever technique you prefer.

Hand Appliqué

Because the center circles have been pressed, with the edges securely turned under, it is easy to hand appliqué. Use a fine, long needle (a #11 Sharp is recommended) and regular or fine machine embroidery thread in a color that will blend with the fabric. This will help make the stitches nearly invisible. Use a single strand no longer than 18 inches.

1. Knot the thread and bring the needle up from the wrong side of the block, just catching the folded edge of the circle.

2. Insert the needle back down into the plate and bring it up again, catching the folded edge about ⅛" away. Continue to stitch around the circle.

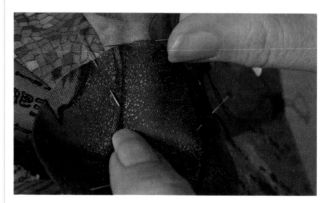

Hand appliqué the center circle to the block.

Invisible Machine Appliqué

Many of our quilts have been made attaching the centers with a monofilament thread on the top and a fine regular thread on the bottom. This gives the look of hand appliqué in much less time. Use the blind stitch or hemming stitch on your machine.

_____/_____/_____/_____

Blind stitch

Refer to your sewing machine manual for details on the blind stitch, checking for the correct needle position and specific recommendations for blind stitching. You'll want to select a stitch that sews a few straight stitches, then one zigzag stitch to the left. Sew in a clockwise direction. Adjust the stitch length and width so that the zigzag stitch catches just a few threads of the circle. Practice on scrap fabrics until you are happy with the results.

✽ Note from Blanche & Lynette

If you have any problems with puckering when you do machine appliqué, try a stabilizer underneath your fabrics. Use a very lightweight interfacing or one of the tear-away stabilizers designed for machine appliqué. We do not use a stabilizer, but some quilters may find it helpful.

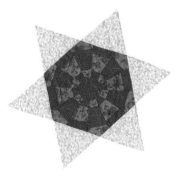

Machine Appliqué with a Decorative Stitch

You can use the overlock stitch, the blanket stitch, satin stitch, or other decorative stitches on your sewing machine to do machine appliqué. The stitching can be done in thread colors that coordinate with each block color; for example, use blue thread for the blue blocks, green thread for the green blocks, etc. For *In My Thirties Garden*, on page 34, the same cream-colored thread was used in an overlock stitch for the appliquéd center in all the blocks. The reproduction prints were pastel enough that the same thread color worked well with all of them. You can also use a contrasting thread color if you want the stitches to show up and be a design element in your quilt. Your sewing machine may have several fun decorative stitches that would work. Make sure that the stitch holds the edge of the center circle securely.

Shell edge stitch or blanket stitch

Overlock stitch

Blanket stitch on a center circle

Cutting Charts

The following three charts give the number of strips and patches to cut for each template size. Use as many different fabrics as possible for the A and B templates. For the flower centers, template C, you can use scraps, or start out with strips if you want your flower centers to be from the same fabric.

Cutting for SMALL Templates: 5½" Block

Quilt Size	# of Blocks	Strip Width	# Strips to Cut		# Patches to Cut
			21" long	42" long	
Baby Quilt 42" x 50"	86	3½"	86	43	516 Template A 516 Template B
		2"	5	3	86 Template C
Twin/Full 65" x 85"	215	3½"	184	92	1290 Template A 1290 Template B
		2"	13	8	215 Template C

Cutting for MEDIUM Templates: 8" Block

Quilt Size	# of Blocks	Strip Width	# Strips to Cut		# Patches to Cut
			21" long	42" long	
Baby Quilt 39" x 45"	28	4½"	39	19	168 Template A 168 Template B
		3"	6	3	28 Template C
Twin/Full 65" x 75"	86	4½"	110	55	516 Template A 516 Template B
		3"	14	7	86 Template C
Queen 91" x 105"	176	4½"	222	111	1056 Template A 1056 Template B
		3"	28	14	176 Template C

Cutting for LARGE Templates: 10" Block

Quilt Size	# of Blocks	Strip Width	# Strips to Cut		# Patches to Cut
			21" long	42" long	
Baby Quilt 50" x 55"	23	6"	40	20	138 Template A 138 Template B
		4"	6	3	23 Template C
Twin/Full 68" x 87"	46	6"	76	38	276 Template A 276 Template B
		4"	12	6	46 Template C
Queen 86" x 112"	77	6"	125	63	462 Template A 462 Template B
		4"	18	9	77 Template C

To estimate the number of A and B patches you can cut from 21" or 42" strips, use the chart below.

Yield Chart for Templates A and B

Templates	Strip Width	Yield from 21" Strip	Yield from 42" Strip
Small Templates A and B	3½"	7 A and 7 B	14 A and 14 B
Medium Templates A and B	4½"	5 A and 5 B	10 A and 10 B
Large Templates A and B	6"	4 A and 4 B	8 A and 8 B

Setting and Border Options

Now for the really fun part! Use a design wall, if you have one, to arrange your blocks. If you don't have a design wall, use the top of a bed. Be spontaneous! Be haphazard! Randomly place the blocks in vertical rows, and then rearrange them until you decide on the look you want. Choose from several setting options and even more border possibilities, and you'll have almost unlimited variations when designing your own quilt.

Settings

There are several ways to set your blocks, the simplest being side-by-side, or rather nested up next to each other. The other possibilities include using equilateral triangles to create the look of a star around each block, and using the triangles to create diamonds in either horizontal or vertical rows. These are the three basic variations that we cover in this chapter, although you can vary these settings as desired. Look at the photographs of quilts throughout the book for even more inspiration.

Side-by-Side Setting

Star Setting

Diamond Setting

SIDE-BY-SIDE SETTING

For this setting, arrange your blocks in vertical rows on a design wall or on a bed. There should always be an odd number of rows so the finished quilt is symmetrical. The blocks will be offset from row to row, so that they "nest" together side-by-side. You will probably not want two similar blocks right next to each other. Have fun playing with different arrangements until you are happy with the results.

Sewing the Blocks Together

Once you've decided on an arrangement that you like, pin a number to the top block of each vertical row. This will help you remember which row is which. Stack the blocks in each vertical row, having the block with the pinned number on top. You will first sew the blocks together into vertical rows.

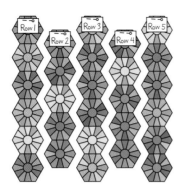

Number the vertical rows.

1. Begin with the numbered block on top of the stack. Align the straight edge with the second block in the stack. Begin stitching ¼" in from the corner. Take 2 or 3 stitches and backstitch the same number of stitches. Continue stitching, ending ¼" from the opposite corner or end. Backstitch to secure the seam. The seam allowances must be free in order to sew the rows together.

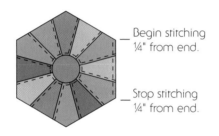

Begin stitching ¼" from end.

Stop stitching ¼" from end.

Backstitch at beginning and ending of seam.

2. Pick up the third block in the row, and stitch in the same manner.

3. Continue to sew blocks together until each row is complete. Press the seam allowances all in one direction.

Sewing the Rows Together

To sew the vertical rows together, treat each straight edge as a separate seam, as you did when sewing blocks together. You will start and stop sewing ¼" from each edge.

1. Align the two edges to be sewn and pin, matching the seams.

2. Begin sewing ¼" away from the edge, backstitch, and continue stitching. Stop ¼" from the edge, and backstitch. Repeat for each straight edge.

Straight Sides versus Angled Sides

After the rows are sewn together, you will have zigzag sides, and an uneven top and bottom that reflects the block shapes. You can choose to stop there, and simply bind your quilt. See the quilt *Dresden Delight* on page 38 for an example of this approach. You can trim blocks or add half blocks to create a straight top and bottom on your quilt. You may want straight edges on just two sides (usually the top and bottom edges), on all four, or none at all!

Another way to achieve straight sides is to add triangles to the outer blocks and then trim them. Or you can appliqué the blocks to a border for straight sides. Read on to see the options, and see also "Borders" beginning on page 24.

✳ *Making Half Blocks*

The best and most accurate way to create the half blocks is to make a complete block and then cut it in half. Blanche doesn't make half blocks. She says, "I hold services, and then cut in two!" You will need to find the center, from point to point. Then cut ¼" away to add the seam allowance. For the star or diamond setting, find the center of the block from flat side to flat side. Then cut ¼" away to add the seam allowance.

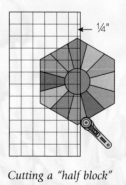

¼"

Cutting a "half block"

STAR SETTING

It is very easy to create a star-like setting. You simply add triangles to opposite sides of the blocks. Make a triangle template in the size needed using the pattern on page 62. See "Making Templates" on page 12 for specific instructions on making templates.

Cutting and Sewing the Triangles

To cut the triangles from strips, see the chart below for strip widths and the number of triangles that you can cut from a 21" strip and from a 42" strip.

1. Place the template on the wrong side of the strip, trace around it with a pencil or fabric marker, rotate the template, and continue drawing across the strip.

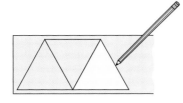

Mark around the triangle on a strip.

2. Use your rotary cutter and ruler to cut the triangles. You can layer your strips to cut more than one triangle at a time without marking each layer of fabric.

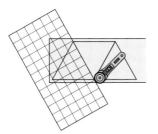

Cut with a rotary cutter and ruler on the drawn lines.

Triangle Cutting Chart

Template D	Strip Width	Yield from 21" Strip	Yield from 42" strip
Small Triangle	3¾"	8	17
Medium Triangle	5¼"	6	13
Large Triangle	6½"	5	9

3. With right sides together, align a triangle with one edge of the block. Stitch, using a ¼" seam allowance. Stitch a second triangle to the opposite end of the block as shown. Press the seam allowances toward the triangles.

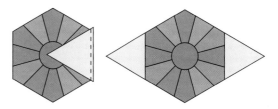

Stitch a triangle to one edge of a block. Stitch another triangle to the opposite edge of the block.

4. Repeat for each block.

Arranging the Blocks

1. Use a design wall or bed to place the blocks in vertical rows, staggering them from row to row. For this setting, you must have an odd number of vertical rows. Don't worry about the triangles at this point. Extra triangles will be removed later. Rearrange the blocks until you are pleased with the arrangement. The outer rows, and every other row will have one more block than each of the even-numbered rows. Refer to the project directions for specific numbers of blocks and rows.

2. Once you are happy with the arrangement, remove triangles as needed from the outer edges of some of the blocks. You will need to add triangles to some blocks to complete the design; some of the blocks will then have three triangles attached. You will need to do this on both the top and bottom of the quilt.

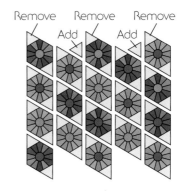

Remove and add triangles as needed.

Assembling the Rows

1. To sew the block units into vertical rows, pin at the intersection of the block and the triangle, so the seams match. Because you have pressed toward the triangles, the seams should naturally butt up against each other, which will aid in sewing perfect seam intersections.

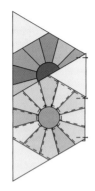

Pin at the seam intersections.

2. Stitch, using a ¼" seam allowance. Continue sewing the block units together to form the rows. Press the rows from the right side, with the seams in one direction. Press each row in alternating directions.

Sew blocks together to make the rows.

3. Sew the rows together, pinning to match the seams.

DIAMOND SETTING

To create a Diamond setting, sew triangles to the blocks as in the Star setting.

1. Lay the blocks out side-by-side, rather than staggered, to create either horizontal or vertical rows of diamonds.

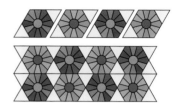

Horizontal rows of blocks create vertical rows of diamonds.

2. Sew the blocks into rows and press the seam allowances in the same direction. Press in the opposite direction from row to row.

3. Sew the rows together, and press the seams in the same direction.

Borders

There are several options for bordering your Dresden Flower Garden quilt. They range from no border at all—simply binding the edges of the quilt—to adding pieced and shaped borders, with or without piping.

NO BORDERS

These quilts can look stunning without borders. It gives them an old-fashioned or contemporary look, depending on the fabric and color choices. Quilters in the past who were truly working with scraps often didn't have large pieces of fabric for borders, so they did not add them. The quilt *Dresden Delight* on page 38 was simply bound around the edges of the blocks. Refer to "Bias Binding" on page 30 for further instructions on binding the angled edges.

APPLIQUÉ ONTO A BORDER

Appliquéing your quilt top onto a border is an easy way to maintain the angled edges of your "flower garden" and keep each block intact and visible, while still creating a quilt with straight sides. See the quilts *Wildflower Bouquet* and *Mattie's Garden* on page 39. Both of these quilts were appliquéd onto either a background or a border.

Your border will need to accommodate the zigzag edges of your quilt and frame it nicely. The end use of the quilt may also help determine the border width. You may want the quilt to fit a certain bed or have a specific amount of overhang. Look at your quilt top and determine whether a border will enhance the composition of the quilt or if it looks great as is.

To add borders, first decide how wide you want the border or borders to be. Lay your border fabric under the pieced center to decide the ultimate width. Blanche sometimes lets the amount of fabric she has determine the border width. You can choose to appliqué first to a fabric that will act as a background, as in *Wildflower Bouquet* and then add borders, or you can add just one fabric to serve as the border.

1. To determine the width to cut the borders, measure from the innermost point along the zigzag edges or angled top and bottom. Measure out to the finished width and then add approximately 6". This will cover the seam allowances and give you a few inches underneath the quilt top for stability when appliquéing. It will also allow you to trim the border and square it up after quilting and before binding.

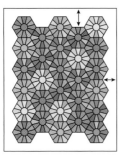

Measure from inner points to determine border width.

2. To determine the length to cut the top and bottom borders, measure the width of the quilt at the widest point through the center. Cut the borders to that length.

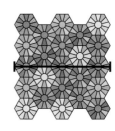

Measure through the center at the widest point.

3. Press the edges of the blocks under ¼" along the top and bottom outer edges. Place the quilt onto the borders, and pin in place along the edges.

> ✳ *Tip from Blanche & Lynette*
> To help press the ¼" seam allowance under the edges of the blocks, we use cardstock as a straight edge. Fold the block edges over the cardstock ¼", add a touch of spray starch, and press. This will keep the edges stable.

4. Machine appliqué the quilt to the border with monofilament thread using the blind stitch. Use a clear thread for light fabrics and a smoke colored thread for dark fabrics. Refer to "Invisible Machine Appliqué" on page 19 for further details if needed.

5. Cut away the excess fabric from the border underneath the pieced blocks, leaving a ¼" seam allowance.

6. To determine the length to cut the side borders, measure the quilt top through the center from top to bottom, including the borders you just added. Cut the side borders to that length.

7. Repeat steps 3 through 5 to appliqué the quilt to the side borders. Appliqué the top and bottom borders to the side border along with the blocks.

Piping

Piping can be added as a decorative accent around the edges of the blocks, around the edge of the quilt next to the binding, or even as a binding. On the quilt, *One Black Sheep* on page 45, piping was used both around the edges of the plates, and also as the binding. On the quilts *Sparkling Stars* and *Midnight Jewel* on pages 44 and 58, piping was used as the binding around the edges of the curved border.

Follow the instructions here to make your own piping. Purchase cotton cording in the size you prefer. We usually use ¼" cording. To use piping as a binding, follow the steps below to make the piping, then refer to "Blanche's Piped Binding" on page 29. Sew the piping to the quilt top before layering and basting it for quilting.

1. Cut 1½"-wide bias strips from the piping fabric. For thicker cording, increase the width of the bias strips. See "Bias Binding" on page 30 for Blanche's method of cutting bias strips and sewing them together.

2. Sew the bias strips together end to end as shown on page 31 to obtain the length needed to go around the edge of the quilt, plus approximately 12" extra.

3. Lay the cording in the center of the bias strips, and fold the bias strip in half wrong sides together encasing the cording and having the raw edges even. Use a zipper foot to stitch close to the cording. Keep the raw edges of the bias strips together, so the cording stays in the center of the piping.

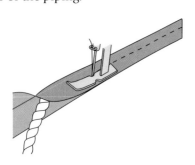

Sew piping inside the fabric strip.

4. Trim the excess fabric from the piping, leaving at least ¼" for a seam allowance.

5. Stitch the piping to the edges of the quilt, as you would sew on a binding. Stitch ¼" from the quilt edge using the zipper foot. The stitching on the piping should be just inside your sewing line so that you will not see the stitching on the piping. At the "peaks" and "valleys," cut into the seam allowance to allow the piping to ease in, yet not lose the shape of the edges.

6. Stop stitching 2" from the point where the ends of the piping will overlap. Cut the end of the piping 1" beyond the beginning end. Remove some stitches from each end of the piping, exposing the cording. Cut the cording so it just meets the other end of the cording. Fold over ½" fabric on the raw end of the piping. Overlap the folded end over the beginning edge and finish machine stitching the piping to the quilt.

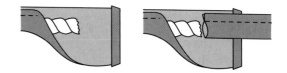

Cut cording and fold end over. Overlap the ends.

Piping with a Border

To add piping around the edges of the blocks and then appliqué to a border, follow the "Piping" instructions above. Sew the piping to the edges of the blocks, and turn under the raw edges. It will then be ready for appliquéing onto a border. See "Appliqué onto a Border" on page 25. Follow up with either a piped or regular binding.

PIECED BORDERS

You can add any type of pieced border to your quilt, of course, but a border that echoes the shapes in the blocks is especially appropriate and can further highlight the design. The pieced borders in the quilts *Rhapsody in Blue* on page 41 and *Strip Heaven* on page 53 are made from the same wedge-shaped pieces as those in the blocks. The border will look best if you use the same template B as you used in your blocks.

Close-up details of wedge-pieced borders

To estimate the number of wedge shapes you'll need to cut for a border, use the formulas below. Measure the length of the border and divide by the number given. Round the answer to the nearest whole number for the approximate number of pieces you'll need to cut using template B.

Small B Template:

Border length divided by .91 = # of B patches to cut

Medium B Template:

Border length divided by 1.35 = # of B patches to cut

Large B Template:

Border length divided by 1.71 = # of B patches to cut

APPLIQUÉD VINE BORDER

The quilt, *Mattie's Garden* on page 39, features a border with a machine appliquéd vine and "petals" using the small size A and B templates.

1. To create the vine, cut bias strips 1½" wide. Join them together with a diagonal seam to obtain the length needed for your quilt border. Refer to "Bias Binding" on page 30 for instructions on cutting and piecing bias strips.

2. Fold in half with wrong sides together and press.

3. Pin the vine to the border, using the photo on page 39 as a placement guide. Machine stitch to the border, stitching about ⅛" from the raw edges.

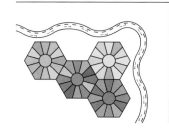

Stitch ⅛" from the raw edges.

4. Fold the vine over, covering the raw edges, and machine appliqué with the blind stitch. See "Invisible Machine Appliqué" on page 19 for further details.

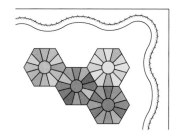

Blind stitch the folded edge.

5. Cut the petals using both the A and B templates. Fold the seam allowances under and press, using spray starch if desired. Pin the shapes in place. Machine appliqué with a satin stitch using a stabilizer underneath to prevent puckering.

Appliqué with a machine satin stitch.

Finishing the Dresden Flower Garden Quilt

Now that your quilt top is complete, you'll need to decide how you want to quilt it and whether or not you need to mark your quilt. If you choose quilting designs that need to be marked on the quilt top, it's best to do that before layering. Then prepare the backing and choose a batting.

Backing

Plan on making the backing a minimum of 2" to 4" larger than the quilt top on all sides. Prewash the fabric, and trim the selvages before you piece.

Batting

The type of batting to use is a personal decision; consult your local quilt shop for suggestions if needed. We prefer low-loft cotton batting to get a more old-fashioned look. Cut the batting approximately 4" larger on all sides than your quilt top for bed size quilts. For wall hangings and crib quilts, 2" larger on all sides is sufficient.

Layering

Spread the backing wrong side up and tape the edges down with masking tape. (If you are working on carpet you can use T-pins to secure the backing to the carpet.) Center the batting on top, smoothing out any folds. Place the quilt top right side up on top of the batting and backing, making sure it's centered.

Basting

If you plan to machine quilt, pin baste the quilt layers together with safety pins placed a minimum of 3" to 4" apart. Begin basting in the center and move toward the edges first in vertical, then horizontal, rows.

If you plan to hand quilt, baste the layers together with thread using a long needle and light-colored thread. Knot one end of the thread. Using stitches approximately the length of the needle, begin in the center and baste out toward the edges.

Quilting

Quilting, whether by hand or machine, should enhance the piecing and appliqué of the quilt. You may choose to quilt in-the-ditch, echo the pieced blocks, use patterns from quilting design books and stencils, or do your own free-motion quilting. One of our favorite ways to quilt the Dresden Flower Garden is to quilt in a continuous line as shown below. This quilting design creates a fun and easy daisy and works well with the wildflower bouquet theme of the quilts.

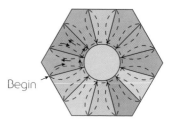

Continuous line daisy design, connecting at the center

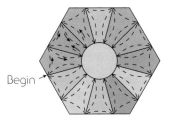

Begin

Continuous line quilting design, connecting at outer edges

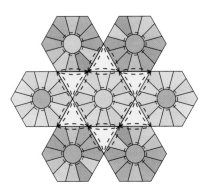

Continuous line quilting design for the Star Variation

On the smallest size block, quilting around each center circle and in the ditch around each block is easy and effective. There are many good machine quilting books on the market today that offer quilting design suggestions. Look for designs that have six sides or will work inside a hexagon. Several of our quilts were quilted in an allover pattern of meandering lines or loops. The quilt *Rose Garden* on page 51 features machine quilted roses centered in each block, with connected roses in the background diamonds. There are many floral quilting designs that would be wonderful with these quilts. Look at the photographs of quilts throughout the book to get other ideas.

Binding

For quilts with straight sides, a double fold, or French fold, binding made from strips cut across the width of the fabric will work well. When binding the edges of the quilts without a border, or binding a quilt with curved edges, use a bias binding. Refer to "Bias Binding" on page 30.

Refer to "Piping" on page 26 to make the length needed.

✱ *Blanche's Piped Binding*

To create a piped binding, refer to "Piping" on page 26 to make the length needed. Attach the piping as you would a binding, but stitch it to the quilt before layering, basting, and quilting. After quilting, trim the backing to ¼" from the edge of the quilt. Trim the batting even with the quilt top. Fold the backing under ¼" and hand stitch it to the flat part of the piping.

DOUBLE FOLD BINDING

1. Trim excess batting and backing from the quilt. Cut the binding fabric into strips 2¼" wide. Piece together with a diagonal seam to make a continuous binding strip.

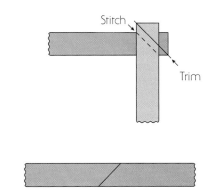

Stitch

Trim

Stitch the strips with a diagonal seam.

2. Press the seams open, then press the entire strip in half lengthwise with wrong sides together. Fold the end of the binding ¼" to the inside and press. With raw edges even, pin the binding to the front edge of the quilt a few inches away from the corner. Leave the first inch of the binding unattached, and begin sewing, using a ¼" seam allowance.

3. Stop ¼" away from the first corner, backstitch one stitch. Lift the presser foot and needle. Rotate the quilt one quarter turn. Fold the binding at a right angle so it extends straight above the quilt. Then fold the binding strip down even with the edge of the quilt. Begin sewing at the folded edge.

Stitch to ¼" from corner.

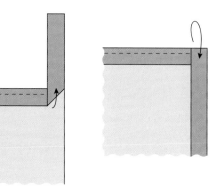

First fold for miter. Second fold alignment. Repeat in the same manner at all corners.

4. Continue stitching around the quilt. Stitch about 1" beyond the folded edge where you started. Clip the threads, remove the quilt from the machine, and trim the excess binding.

5. Fold the binding over the raw edges to the back of the quilt, and hand stitch, mitering the corners as you come to them.

BIAS BINDING

If you choose to bind around the uneven or "zigzag" edges of your quilt, without adding a border, a bias binding works best. It will give you extra flexibility in mitering the outer points and pivoting at the inner points.

Making the Bias Binding

1. To cut the strips for a bias binding, begin by squaring up the cut edges of your fabric.

2. Fold your fabric diagonally, bringing a selvage even with a cut edge, then fold again diagonally.

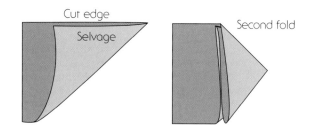

Fold the fabric for bias binding.   Fold the fabric a second time.

3. Cut a straight line close to the double-folded edge and then cut strips at 2¼" increments.

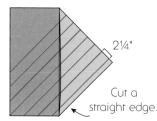

Cut 2¼" strips for binding.

4. Trim the selvages off by cutting across the strip at a 45° angle.

Cut the ends of the bias strips at a 45° angle.

5. Sew the strips end to end using a ¼" seam allowance with right sides together. Create one long binding strip, and press the seam allowances open. The angled seams keep the bulk of the seam allowances evenly distributed.

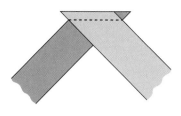

Sew the bias strips together.

6. Lay one end of the binding strip right side down on an ironing surface, with the tip of the angle to the right. Press a ⅜" or ¼" hem along the edge. Press the strip in half lengthwise with wrong sides together.

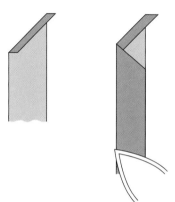

Press hem on one end of binding.   Press the strip in half.

🌼 *Note from Blanche*

Staystitch a scant ¼" away from the raw edges of the binding to help avoid ruffling of the binding when sewing the binding to the quilt.

Attaching the Binding

Use a walking foot or a dual feed mechanism if you have one for your machine. It will help to feed the layers evenly through the machine when stitching the binding.

1. Working from the right side of the quilt, lay the binding on the quilt. Begin in the middle of a block edge. Line up the raw edges of the quilt top with the raw edge of the binding. Sew just to the left of the line of staystitching, using a ¼" seam.

2. Along the uneven zigzag edges of the plates, you will need to do a very small miter on the "peaks," or outer points of the blocks. Stop stitching ¼" from the point and backstitch. Lift the presser foot and needle. Rotate the quilt, fold the binding back, and then align it even with the next edge of the quilt. Begin sewing at the folded edge.

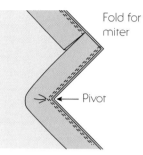

Miter the outer points and pivot at inside corners.

3. To pivot at the inner points, or "valleys," stop stitching ¼" from the two raw edges of the corner, and with the needle down, pivot around the corner.

4. Continue stitching around the quilt. Stitch about 1" beyond the folded hem edge where you started. Clip the threads, remove the quilt from the machine, and trim the excess binding. Clip into the seam allowance at the inner points and trim excess fabric at the points to minimize bulk.

5. Fold the binding over the raw edges to the back of the quilt, and hand stitch, mitering the corners as you come to them.

The Last Details

Add a label with your name, date, and hometown so that no one will ever have to wonder who made that incredible quilt! Add a hanging sleeve if the quilt will be hung on the wall.

The Quilts

The Basic Quilt:
In My
Thirties Garden

Quilt size: 48" x 48"

Finished block size: 5½"

Number of blocks: 45

We call this the basic quilt because it is the simplest setting. The blocks are sewn next to each other, showcasing the wildflower bouquet look unique to this design. This quilt features reproduction prints from the 1930s. Like many quilters, Lynette just loves those fabrics, and they make wonderful baby quilts. With eight grandchildren age five and under, she has made her fair share of them over the past few years! Surrounding the pastel wildflower garden is a charming white picket fence border. The corners feature appliquéd medium size blocks.

In My
Thirties Garden

48" x 48". *Pieced and machine quilted by Lynette Young Bingham, 2002.*

Fabrics

- Fat quarters (18 to 36) or small amounts of at least 6 to 12 different 1930s reproduction prints *in each of the following colors:* pink, purple, blue, green, peach, and yellow for the blocks and block centers

- 1 yard white tone-on-tone ivy, leaf, or floral print for fence and corner squares

- 5/8 yard green print for border

- 3 yards fabric for backing

- 3/8 yard fabric for binding

- Batting, 54" x 54"

Templates

Use the SMALL A, B, and C templates to make this project as shown. You will also need the MEDIUM A, B, and C templates to make the appliquéd corner blocks. Refer to "Making Templates" on page 12 if you will be making your own. Use the patterns on pages 61 and 62.

Cutting

Blocks

From the block fabrics, cut: 39 strips, 3½" x 21"; cut 270 A patches and 270 B patches (45 of each template from each of the six colors).

MAKE IT TWIN SIZE

A twin-size version of this quilt would be lovely in a young girl's bedroom or in a guest room. Make it in sherbet-colored pastel fabrics, in bright jewel tone colors, or whatever suits the recipient. Here are the basics.

Size: 72" x 82" or 72" x 92"*

Finished block size: 8"

Number of blocks: 71

Templates:
Use the Medium A, B, and C templates

*Note: The smaller dimensions include a picket fence border on the sides and bottom only. The longer size includes a picket fence on all four sides.

Fabrics

5 yards total for blocks

2 yards white tone-on-tone ivy, leaf, or floral print for fence and corner squares

1⅛ yards green print for border

5½ yards fabric for backing

¾ yard fabric for binding

Batting, 78" x 89" or 78" x 98"

Make 71 medium blocks, and follow the instructions for the wall hanging. Set the blocks in 7 vertical rows. Rows 1, 3, 5, 7 each have ten blocks, and Rows 2, 4, 6 each have nine blocks. Trim Rows 1, 3, 5, 7 to make a straight edge along the top if you will not add the picket fence border; do not trim the bottom edge until after the fence is appliquéd.

For the picket fence border make 4 strip sets (from 8 green and 4 white strips). You will need 36 units for the sides (18 each side: 9 white and 9 pieced), and 26 units for the top and bottom borders (13 each side: 6 white and 7 pieced). Cut a total of 30 pickets and 32 pieced background/crossbar units at 4½" to finish at 4". For a fence border on just three sides, cut 24 pickets and 25 pieced background units.

From each of the six different color block fabrics, cut: 4 rectangles, 4½" x 5"; layer several of these rectangles and cut 1 Medium Template A and B patch from each.

From the block fabrics, cut: 45 circles using Small Template C

4 circles using Medium Template C

Picket Fence Border

From the white fabric, cut:

5 strips, 3" x 42"; cut into

20 rectangles, 3" x 10"

2 strips, 2" x 42"

4 squares, 10¾" x 10¾"

From the green print, cut:

4 strips, 4½" x 42"

Binding

From the binding fabric, cut:

5 strips, 2¼" x 42"

Quilt Construction

MAKING THE BLOCKS

1. Refer to "Sewing the Blocks" on page 15 to make 7 or 8 blocks in each of the six colors, for a total of 45 blocks.

2. Refer to "The Flower Centers" on page 17 to add the centers to each of the blocks.

ARRANGING THE BLOCKS

1. Use a design wall or bed to place the blocks in seven vertical rows, staggering the blocks as shown.

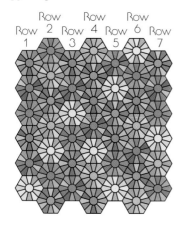

Placement of the blocks

2. Refer to "Sewing the Blocks Together" on page 21 to sew seven vertical rows. Rows One, Three, Five, and Seven each have six blocks, and Rows Two, Four, and Six each have seven blocks.

3. Refer to "Sewing the Rows Together" on page 22 to sew the rows together. The top and bottom blocks on the even-numbered rows will be partially under the appliquéd picket fence border, so leave them intact for now.

PIECING THE BORDER

1. Use a ¼" seam allowance, and sew a 4½" x 42" strip of green background fabric to either side of a 2" x 42" white strip. Make two of these strip sets. Press seams toward the green fabric.

2. Cut the strip sets into 3" wide units. You will need 24 units.

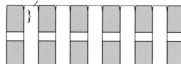

Make two strip sets, and cut into 3" units.

3. With right sides together, stitch one of the pieced units from step 2 to one 3" x 10" white rectangle. Begin stitching 1½" in from the picket edge. Alternately sew pieced units and white rectangles until there are five white "pickets" and six pieced background rectangles. Make 4 of these border sections.

Make 4 border sections.

ATTACHING THE BORDER

1. Begin on one side of the quilt, where there is an even "zigzag" along the edge. Work on a flat surface, and place the pieced fence border on top of the edge of the quilt. Place the center white picket at the center point between the third and fourth blocks.

2. Fold and finger press the edges of the center white picket to a point and pin to the seam between the two center blocks. Pin along the edge as necessary, overlapping ¼" onto the right side of the blocks. The pickets are appliquéd on top of the blocks, while the green pieced segments go underneath the blocks. The 1½" that was left free in the sewing is what you will be tucking under and over as you fold and pin along the edge.

3. Fold and finger press the edges of the blocks on top of the green background, centering on the green fabric. Pin along the edges.

4. Continue folding, finger pressing, and pinning along the edge, alternating the pickets on top of the blocks, and the blocks on top of the green fabric between the pickets.

Fold under to create a point.

Placement of fence border

5. Refer to "Hand Appliqué" on page 18 for instructions to hand appliqué the edges of the picket fence border to the quilt. If you prefer to do appliqué by machine, see "Invisible Machine Appliqué" on page 19 and use the blind stitch.

6. Repeat Steps 1 through 5 to appliqué the border to the opposite side.

7. The other sides do not have the even zigzag edges and have approximately half a block extra in every other row. The borders for these two sides will be appliquéd on top of the blocks. Fold, press, and pin the picket points and the green background onto the blocks, keeping the edge straight between the pickets.

8. Appliqué the borders to the quilt center.

9. From the wrong side of the quilt, carefully trim the excess fabric from the border and the blocks to ¼".

FINISHING THE CORNERS

Because of variances in seam allowances, you may have to adjust the size of your corner square to accommodate your quilt. It was cut slightly oversized and may need to be trimmed before or after sewing.

1. Place the corner square, right sides together, on one end of the pieced border, aligning the raw edges. Stitch with a ¼" seam allowance. Press toward the green background fabric.

2. Lay the entire corner of the quilt flat, to see if the other side seam of the corner square can be sewn with a ¼" seam, or if any adjustments need to be made so the corner will lay flat. Don't worry if there is a gap at the inside corner block; the block will be appliquéd onto the corner square.

3. Sew the seam to attach the corner square to the pieced green background on the other side. Repeat for the other corners. Trim seam allowances to ¼" if needed.

4. Lay the quilt flat again to pin the raw edge of each block at the corners onto each corner square. Fold the edges under, finger press, and appliqué in place as shown.

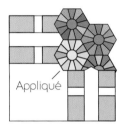

Sew the side seams, then appliqué the edges of the quilt top onto the corner square.

Appliquéd Corner Blocks

1. Make 4 medium blocks referring to "Sewing the Blocks" on page 15. In the quilt shown in the photo, two patches each of the six colors were placed side by side around the block. A different color center circle is sewn onto each block.

2. Fold and finger press the edges of the block under ¼". Center one block on each corner square. Pin and appliqué the blocks.

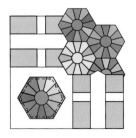

Appliqué the medium block to the corner square.

Quilting

Refer to "Finishing the Dresden Flower Garden Quilt" on page 28. *In My Thirties Garden* was machine quilted around the center circle of each block, and in the ditch along the seam lines around each block. The picket fence border was free-motion quilted on the pickets and crossbars with leafy vines in two different colors of green thread. The medium blocks in each corner were quilted in continuous line arcs resembling petals, as shown on page 28.

Binding

Refer to "Binding" on page 29 to bind the quilt.

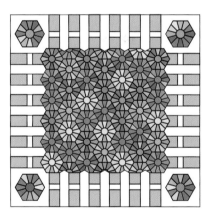

Quilt Layout

Gallery Quilts

Posey Patch 1998

46½" x 53"

Small blocks; pieced and machine quilted by Blanche Young.

The quilt top is appliquéd onto a striped background fabric, and a striped border print creates the border.

Dresden Delight 1998

64" x 89½"

Medium blocks; pieced and machine quilted by Blanche Young.

The teals and orange-reds really sparkle in this delightful quilt, bound around the uneven outer edges.

Stained Glass Window 1995

71½" x 103"

Large blocks; pieced and machine quilted by Blanche Young.

The wide stained glass border fabric provides a dramatic frame for this quilt, which appears to be lit from within.

Wildflower Bouquet 1999

42" x 52"

Small blocks; pieced and machine quilted by Blanche Young.

Similar to *Posey Patch* (see previous page), this wall hanging features a different number of blocks and rows to create a different size quilt. The quilt top is appliquéd onto a wider background and the border is a wider striped border print.

Mattie's Garden 2002

99" x 104"

Large blocks; pieced and machine appliquéd by Blanche Young, machine quilted by Marian Gallian.

This quilt is named for Blanche's mother and Lynette's grandmother, Elnora Mattie Day Stringfellow Boberg. Mattie was a master gardener; her beautiful flowerbeds and gardens were her pride and joy. Blanche learned color basics from her mother and her flower gardens. The highlight of this gorgeous quilt is a machine appliquéd vine border with petals cut from the small A and B templates.

Star Variation:
Rhapsody
in Blue

Quilt size: 66" x 93"
Finished block size: 10"
Number of blocks: 38

Blanche delved into her stash of blues, greens, and turquoise to make this wonderful quilt. It showcases light, medium, and dark values of both turquoise blues and true-blue colors of fabrics in the blocks. Hints of red, gold, and orange add just the right amount of spark. The background triangles are made from a light print, but a dark fabric would also work well (see *Sparkling Stars* on page 44). Just be sure that you have a good contrast between the triangle fabric and the blocks. The "star" design is created when triangles are sewn on opposite ends of each block, and the blocks are sewn together in vertical rows.

Rhapsody in Blue features uneven edges on the top and bottom and side borders made from Template B "wedges." Additional background borders were added on either side of the wedge border. Our version was made using the large size blocks, but choose any size for your own stunning interpretation.

66" x 93". Pieced by Blanche Young; machine quilted by Dorothy Barnett, 2001.

Fabrics

- 5 yards total of medium and dark fabrics (scraps and fat quarters) for the blocks

- ½ yard total or scraps for the appliquéd block centers

- 2½ yards of light fabric for the triangles and border strips

- 1½ yards total of medium and dark fabrics for the pieced wedge border

- 6 yards fabric for backing

- ¾ yard fabric for binding

- Batting, 75" x 101"

Templates

Use the LARGE A, B, and C templates to make this project as shown. Refer to "Making Templates" on page 12 if you will be making your own. Use the patterns on pages 61 and 62. You will also need to make a template from the large D triangle pattern found on page 62.

MAKE A CRIB QUILT

This design would be a wonderful and unique baby quilt with the irregular edges on the top and bottom. Use pastels, bright primary colors, or soft muted colors to create a pint-size version. Here's what you'll need for a small rendition.

Quilt size: 50½" x 52"
Finished block size: 5½"
Number of blocks: 53
Templates:
Use the Small A, B, C, and D templates

Fabrics

2¾ yards total of medium and dark fabrics for the blocks
Scraps for the appliquéd block centers
1¼ yards of light fabric for the triangles and border strips (104 triangles)
½ yard total of medium and dark fabrics for the pieced wedge border
3¼ yards fabric for backing
½ yard fabric for binding
Batting, 54" x 56"

Make 53 small blocks and follow the instructions for making the large quilt. The quilt will have 7 vertical rows: Rows 1, 3, 5, and 7 have 8 blocks; Rows 2, 4, and 6 have 7 blocks. You will need approximately 45 B patches (total of 90) for each pieced side border.

Cutting

Blocks

From each of the block fabrics, cut:

1 strip 6"-wide; cut 228 A patches and 228 B patches

From the fabric for the block centers, cut:

38 circles using Template C*

Triangles

From the light fabric, cut:

9 strips, 6½" x 42"; cut 74 triangles using the large Template D

Border

From the wedge border fabrics, cut:

108 B patches

From the light border fabric, cut:

10 strips 2½" x 42"

Binding

From the binding fabric, cut:

9 strips, 2¼" x 42"

*You may want to cut the circles after the blocks are sewn.

Quilt Construction

MAKING THE BLOCKS

1. Refer to "Sewing the Blocks" on page 15 to make 38 large blocks.

2. Refer to "The Flower Centers" on page 17 to add the center to each of the blocks.

3. Refer to "Cutting and Sewing the Triangles" on page 23 to add the triangles to each block.

ARRANGING THE BLOCKS

1. Use a design wall or bed to place the blocks in five vertical rows, staggering the blocks. Rearrange the blocks until you are pleased with the arrangement. Rows One, Three, and Five each have eight blocks, and Rows Two and Four each have seven blocks. Refer to the Quilt Layout at right.

2. Refer to "Arranging the Blocks" on page 23 to create the design as shown in the Quilt Layout.

ASSEMBLING THE ROWS

Refer to "Assembling the Rows" on page 23 to sew the block units into rows.

ADDING BORDERS

This quilt features borders on the sides, consisting of 2" finished-width borders of background fabric on either side of the pieced Template B border.

1. Measure the length of the quilt through the middle of the center row. This will give you enough extra length to allow for the angled edge at the top and bottom. Piece the 2½"-wide strips of the background fabric together to get the length needed. Make a total of four border strips.

2. Sew the B patches together using a ¼" seam allowance; begin sewing at the wide end, and stitch to the narrow end. You can sew them together randomly or lay them out

in a planned arrangement. Each border strip consists of 54 patches. Due to slight variations in individual stitching and seam allowance width, however, you may need one more, or one less patch to make the required strip length for your quilt.

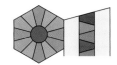

Sew the B patches together.

3. Press all seam allowances in one direction.

4. Sew the 2½"-wide borders to each side of the patchwork border, extending the background fabric beyond the patchwork, so that you can cut the borders at an angle to match the angle of the last B patch, as shown. Press toward the background borders. You may need to adjust seam allowances for the border wedges to come out perfectly. Or you can simply cut through a wedge to maintain the same angle at all the corners.

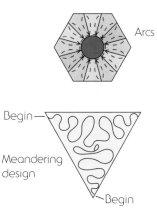

Cut the borders at an angle.

5. Align the border with the quilt center. Pin and sew the border to the quilt. Press toward the borders.

Quilt Layout

Quilting

The quilt shown was machine quilted as shown below with a meandering design in the triangles and background borders. The blocks were quilted in a continuous line design of arcs to create the look of petals.

Arcs

Begin—
Meandering design
└Begin

Binding

Refer to "Bias Binding" on page 30. Bind the quilt, pivoting at the inner corners and making a small miter at the outer points along the zigzag edges.

Gallery Quilts

Sparkling Stars 2001

44" x 57"

Small blocks; pieced and machine quilted by Blanche Young.

Meander quilting with bright primary colored variegated thread picks up the primary colored dots in the background fabric. This wall hanging features an outer border cut and bound in a distinctive shape.

Flamingo Lagoon 2002

60" x 67"

Medium blocks; pieced by Lynette Young Bingham, machine quilted by Marian Gallian.

The blocks and triangles reflect the jewel-toned flamingos in the wide border. The quilting in the border follows the water flow, and the blocks are quilted with a design that works well with the hexagon shape.

Trudy's Green Thumb 2001

72" x 85"

Large blocks; pieced by Carol DeFelice of Temecula, California, machine quilted by Marian Gallian.

Carol made this quilt as a tribute to her mother Trudy Emerich of Redlands, California, for her magical abilities as a gardener. The light fabric print provides a wonderfully contrasting background. Carol used her stash of 500 charm squares (6" x 6") to make this wonderful quilt. She organized the charm squares by color and value. Note that there are very few repeated fabrics. The machine quilting consists of continuous-line loops with scattered flowers and heart-shaped leaves.

One Black Sheep 2001

79" x 87"

Medium blocks; pieced by Blanche Young, machine quilted by Marian Gallian.

Blanche named this quilt for the one black block near the bottom. The piped border creates a unique frame around the uneven edges of the blocks and is finished with a piped binding. The background triangles and border are quilted with continuous line loops, and the blocks are quilted with a sunburst design.

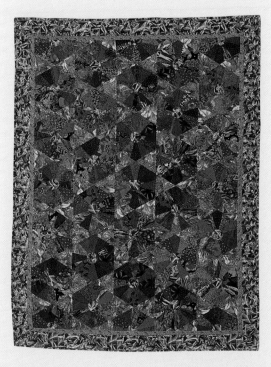

Cow Pies in the Sky 2002

48" x 66"

Medium blocks; pieced and machine quilted by Blanche Young.

Blanche had an idea when she made all these brown blocks, but the finished quilt was not what she had originally envisioned. All the center circles are from the same fabric as the colorful border. When Blanche set all the blocks against a china blue print, Lynette nicknamed the quilt *Cow Pies in the Sky.* Blanche showed this quilt during a lecture, and the audience laughed and cheered. They loved the name—and the quilt!

Diamond Variation:
Red Lanterns

Quilt size: 74" x 95"

Finished block size: 10"

Number of blocks: 35

Red Lanterns is Blanche's solution to making a successful quilt of all red blocks. When she initially set them together side by side, they became a sea of red. Separating the red blocks with the gray triangles and adding a coordinating border print stripe created a very striking design. Although red is the main color, many of the prints contain accent colors—purples, pinks, greens, blues, yellows, and creams. The border print makes a beautiful framed finish for the outer border, and a narrow stripe in the fabric was used between the rows.

Red Lanterns is made up of thirty-five blocks, sewn in seven horizontal rows. The setting uses equilateral triangles to create a vertical row of diamonds interrupted by the horizontal border stripe. The setting can also be done without the horizontal sashing strips, as shown in the quilt *Rose Garden* on page 51. See "Diamond Setting" on page 24 for further instructions.

74" x 95". Pieced by Blanche Young; machine quilted by Marian Gallian, 2001.

Fabrics

- 5 yards total of medium and dark red fabrics for the blocks

- ½ yard total or scraps for the appliquéd block centers

- 2 yards of light fabric for the triangles

- 3 yards striped border print with both wide and narrow stripes

- 7½ yards fabric for backing

- ⅝ yard fabric for binding

- Batting, 82" x 103"

Templates

Use the LARGE A, B, and C templates to make this project as shown. Refer to "Making Templates" on page 12 if you will be making your own. Use the patterns on pages 61 and 62. You will also need to make a template from the Large D triangle template found on page 62.

Cutting

Blocks

From each of the block fabrics, cut:

1 strip, 6" x 42"; cut 210 A patches and 210 B patches.

From the fabric for the block centers, cut:

35 circles using Template C*

DOWNSIZE IT FOR A WALLHANGING

What a fabulous design to hang on a wall. Make it in Japanese fabrics for a stunning accent piece. Or make an impact using just one color as Blanche did here in *Red Lanterns*.

Quilt size: 51" x 53"

Finished block size: 5½"

Number of blocks: 42

Templates:
Use the Small A, B, C, and D templates

Triangles

From the light fabric, cut:

10 strips, 6½" x 42"; cut 84 triangles using the large Template D

Border and Sashing Strips

From the border stripe print, cut:

4 strips, ¼" on either side of the wide stripes the entire length of the fabric (3 yards long)†

4 strips, ¼" on either side of the narrow stripes the entire length of the fabric (3 yards long)‡

Binding

From the binding fabric, cut:

9 strips, 2¼" x 42"

You may want to cut the circles after the blocks are sewn.

Fabrics

2 yards total of medium and dark fabrics for the blocks

Scraps for the appliquéd block centers

¾ yard of light fabric for the triangles (96 triangles)

2 yards border print stripe that has both wide and narrow stripes

3¼ yards fabric for backing

½ yard fabric for binding

Batting, 55" x 57"

Make 42 small blocks and follow the instructions for the large quilt. Set the blocks in 6 horizontal rows of 7 blocks each. Cut the sashing strips 2½" wide, or a width that accommodates the border stripe. Cut the outer borders 4½" wide.

†*The excess length on each strip will be used to miter the corners to frame the quilt.*

‡*Two of the strips will be pieced. if you prefer not to piece them, and there are enough stripes on the fabric, cut six strips of the narrow stripe.*

Quilt Construction

MAKING THE BLOCKS

1. Refer to "Sewing the Blocks" on page 15 to make 35 large blocks.

2. Refer to "The Flower Centers" on page 17 to add the center to each of the blocks.

3. Refer to "Cutting and Sewing the Triangles" on page 23 to add the triangles to each block.

Arranging the Blocks

1. Use a design wall or bed to place the blocks in seven horizontal rows. Don't worry about the triangles at this point. Extra triangles will be added later to fill in the edges of each row. Rearrange the blocks until you are pleased with the arrangement. All the rows will have an equal number of blocks.

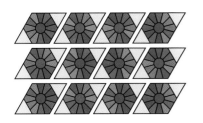

Arrange blocks in rows.

2. Once you are happy with the arrangement, sew a triangle to the upper left edge of the first block and the lower right edge of the last block in each row.

Add a triangle to the end of each row.

Assembling the Quilt

1. To sew the block units into rows, pin at the intersection of the block and the triangle, so the seams match. The seams should butt up against each other, which aids in sewing perfect intersections. Stitch, using a ¼" seam allowance.

Sew the blocks together in rows.

2. Continue sewing the block units together to form the rows. Press the rows from the right side, with the seams going in one direction. Press seams in opposite directions from row to row.

3. You will need to trim the side edges of each row to remove the excess from the outer triangles. Using a ruler, align along the edge, and allow for a ¼" seam allowance, as shown.

Cut a straight edge at row ends.

4. Measure the length of each row through the center to determine the length needed for the horizontal sashing strips. Cut or piece the strips as needed.

5. Using a ¼" seam allowance, stitch the sashing strip to a row of blocks. Stitch with the border print strip on the top, so that you can follow the design on the stripe. This will ensure that the design is consistent on all the rows, and it won't look crooked or uneven.

Stitch along the design edge using a ¼" seam allowance.

6. Continue sewing the sashing strips to join the seven rows. Press toward the sashing strip.

Mitered Outer Border

Striped border prints make a wonderful "frame" for your quilt, especially with mitered corners. Be sure that you center a particular design along each side of the quilt so that all four corners will have the same look when mitered.

1. To determine how long the side border strips need to be, measure the length of the quilt through the center. To this measurement, add two times the width of the cut border strip. Then add 2" for the angled seam. Cut the border strips to that length. For example, if the length of the quilt through the middle is 82", and the border print strip is cut 6½" wide, it would be: 82" + (6½" x 2) = 95" + 2" = 97".

2. Repeat step 1 for the top and bottom borders. Measure the width of the quilt through the middle, then add twice the width of the cut border plus 2". If the quilt is 59" wide, it would be:

$$59" + (6½" \times 2) = 72" + 2" = 74".$$

3. Starting with a side border, fold the border in half end-to-end and mark the center with a pin. From this pin, measure toward each end of the border strip to half the actual length of your quilt. For an 82" long quilt, measure 41" in either direction. Mark these points with pins.

Half of length   Half of length

Center

Mark the borders.

4. Find the center of the quilt sides and pin a border to each side of the quilt, matching the center points of the quilt and the border, and matching the outer pins to the corners of the quilt. Insert additional pins in between, easing in any fullness and keeping the raw edges even.

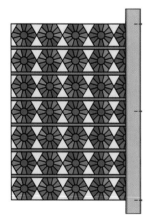

Center the border strip on the quilt.

5. Repeat Step 4 for the top and bottom borders.

6. Begin sewing at one corner of the quilt, with the striped border strip on the top, so that you can follow the design line of the stripe. Start stitching ¼" in from the raw edges of the quilt. Take 3 or 4 stitches and then backstitch 3 stitches. Take care not to stitch into the ¼" seam allowance. Sew the length of the quilt, but stop stitching ¼" from the edge of the quilt, and backstitch.

7. Add the second border in the same way. Work around the quilt in this manner to add the third and fourth borders.

8. Lay one corner of the quilt and border, right side up, on an ironing board. Open the border away from the quilt. Press the seams toward the border. Arrange the excess fabric of the borders to extend straight, lapping the vertical border over the horizontal border. Fold the end of the vertical border under itself at a 45° angle, so the excess fabric of this border lines up with the excess of the other border. Use a ruler with a 45° angle to check that the angle is correct and the corner is square. Press this crease. Pin the excess fabric of the borders together to hold the angle.

Fold

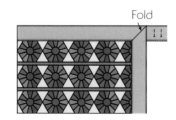

Pin the excess border after folding and pressing the miter.

9. Pick up the quilt by the borders to allow the quilt to fold, right sides together, on the diagonal toward the corner of the quilt. Keep the raw edges of the borders even and sew at the crease of the border, starting at the outside of the borders and stitching toward the corner of the quilt. Stitch to the seam lines and then backstitch. Trim the mitered seam allowance to ⅜" and press the seams open. Press the border seams toward the border.

Stitch

Stitch the mitered corner.

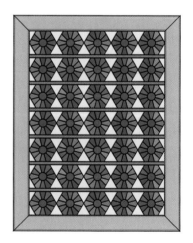

Quilt Layout

Quilting

Red Lanterns was machine quilted in a lovely fleur-de-lis design.

Binding

Refer to "Binding" on page 29 to bind the quilt.

Gallery Quilt

Rose Garden 2002

85" x 96"

Medium blocks; pieced by Blanche Young and Lynette Young Bingham, machine quilted by Marian Gallian.

This stunning quilt also uses a striped border print, but only as the outer border. The border was tea-dyed from a very light off-white to create the perfect beige to match the quilt. The blocks are sewn in vertical rows, so the diamond design goes across the quilt horizontally. The quilting design is a large rose with leaves centered on each block and smaller connected rose trellises in the diamonds.

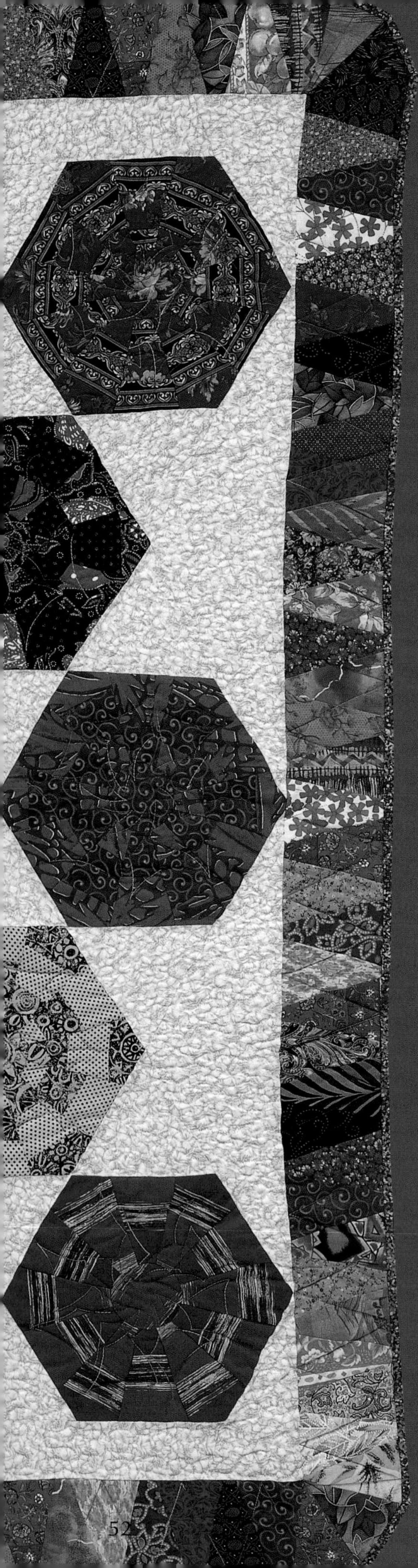

Strip-Pieced Variation:
Strip Heaven

Quilt size: 63" x 93"

Finished block size: 10"

Number of blocks: 33

Strip Heaven is a fun, and wonderfully easy quilt that has the appeal and look of many kaleidoscopes. It looks more complicated than it really is. Each block consists of two fabrics sewn in strips, cut with the Dresden Flower Garden templates and re-sewn to create a fresh new block. Now is your chance to use your stash of stripes and other fabrics that you can't use elsewhere. The blocks are set with triangles, and the quilt has a pieced border made from Template B patches. The continuous line machine quilting in a bold variegated thread is a wild design full of curves and angles—the perfect finish for this quilt.

63" x 93". Pieced by Blanche Young; machine quilted by Marian Gallian, 2001.

Fabrics

- 66 different prints for blocks: Fat quarters, or pieces approximately 8" x 22"

- 2½ yards of light fabric for the triangles and borders

- 2¼ yards total of light, medium and dark fabrics for the pieced wedge border

- 5½ yards fabric for backing

- ⅝ yard fabric for binding

- Batting, 69" x 98"

Templates

Use the LARGE A, B, and C templates to make this project as shown. Refer to "Making Templates" on page 12 if you will be making your own. Use the patterns on pages 61 and 62. You will also need to make a template from the large D triangle pattern found on page 62.

Before You Cut

Before cutting your block fabrics, group them into 33 pairs of light and dark. Be sure to have good contrast between the two fabrics in each pair. This is essential for the design to be effective (refer to photo). You will be making strip sets from three strips of the two different fabrics, alternating the colors in each.

Downsize It for a Wall Hanging

With all the fascinating variations you can get by using strip-pieced blocks, you might want to make a wall hanging size of this quilt. You and your guests can admire the kaleidoscope effects the blocks create as the quilt graces the walls of your home. Here are the basics of downsizing this quilt using the diamond setting as Blanche did in her quilt, *Midnight Jewel*, on page 58.

Quilt size: 40" x 45" (without borders)
Finished block size: 8"
Number of blocks: 25
Templates:
Use the Medium A, B, C, and D templates

For these large blocks, your strip set will need to be at least 6" wide after stitching. Here are some suggested widths for cutting the three strips:

Cut strips 2", 3", and 2"
or
Cut strips 1¾", 3½", and 1¾"

You can stack several pairs together for cutting, depending on how many layers you are comfortable cutting at a time.

Fabrics

50 different prints for blocks: Fat quarters, or pieces approximately 8" x 22"
⅞ yard of light fabric for the triangles (cut 60)
2¾ yards fabric for backing
½ yard fabric for binding
Batting, 44" x 49"

Make 25 medium blocks and follow the instructions for the large quilt to make the strip sets and the blocks. Set the blocks in 5 horizontal rows of 5 blocks each.

When making the medium size blocks, use only two strips (not three) in the strip sets. The sewn strip sets should finish at 4½" wide. Some suggested widths for cutting strips are: 3" and 2", 2½" and 2½", and 3½" and 1½". To make it really simple, cut all your 22" strips 2½" wide and sew them together in strip sets. Simply place the template higher or lower along the strip set to change the look of the finished block. Just be sure that you cut six identical A patches and six identical B patches for each block.

The fun and exciting thing about the strip-pieced variation is that you do not have to cut all your strips the same width. You can experiment with this: stack and cut strips for several blocks, then change the strip width for the next several blocks. This will ensure a good variety of different, interesting blocks. The cutting instructions that follow will give you blocks with two width variations. Feel free to vary the strip width as you like. Adjust your cutting accordingly.

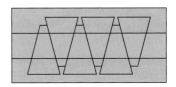

Cutting

Blocks

From each of 17 pairs of light and dark block fabrics, cut:

2 dark strips, 2" x 22"

1 dark strip, 3" x 22"

2 light strips, 2" x 22"

1 light strip, 3" x 22"

From each of 16 pairs of block fabrics, cut:

2 dark strips, 1¾" x 22"

1 dark strip, 3½" x 22"

2 light strips, 1¾" x 22"

1 light strip, 3½" x 22"

From the fabric for the block centers, cut:

33 circles using Template C*

Triangles

From the light fabric, cut:

9 strips, 6½" x 42"; cut 76 triangles using the large Template D

Border

From the wedge border fabrics, cut:

174 B patches

From the light fabric, cut:

5 strips, 3" x 42"

Binding

From the binding fabric, cut:

9 strips, 2¼" x 42"

You may want to cut the circles after the blocks are sewn.

Quilt Construction

MAKING THE STRIP SETS

1. For Strip Set 1, sew two 2" x 22" strips of the light fabric on either side of the contrasting dark 3" x 22" strip. For Strip Set 2, sew two 2" x 22" strips of the contrasting dark fabric on either side of the light 3" x 22" strip. Press toward the outer strips.

[strip set diagram]

Strip Set 1

[strip set diagram]

Strip Set 2

2. Using the large Template A, cut six patches from Strip Set 1 as shown.

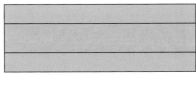

Cut six patches from Strip Set 1.

3. Using the large Template B, cut six patches from Strip Set 2 as shown. You will want to "stagger" the placement of the template on the strip set so it is not lined up with the seams on the patches cut from Strip Set 1. This staggered look is more interesting. If you match your seams, you create "bull's eyes." You can really have

fun with each block by moving the templates up or down the strip sets, *but be sure all six patches for one block are cut exactly the same.*

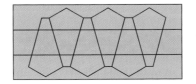

Cut 6 patches from Strip Set 2, staggering the template.

4. Repeat steps 1 through 3 with all the remaining strips cut from the pairs of block fabrics.

MAKING THE BLOCKS

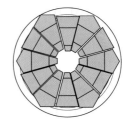

Arrange patches on a paper plate.

1. Refer to "Sewing the Blocks" on page 15 to stitch and press the blocks. Make 33.

2. Refer to "The Flower Centers" on page 17 to cut and appliqué the centers to the blocks.

3. Refer to "Cutting and Sewing the Triangles" on page 23 to add the triangles to each block.

Notes from Blanche

As mentioned before, you can change the width of the strips when you sew the strip sets for a good variety of fabric placement. You can also change the look of the block by moving the templates up or down on the strip set when cutting. For large blocks, be sure the total of the finished strip set is at least 6".

You do not have to have equal size strips on either side of the center strip. Other combinations of suggested strip widths are: 3", 2", 2" and 1½", 3½", 2". When the outer strips are a different width, cut Template A patches with the point at the top for all patches, so they are all identical, as shown.

Outer strips are not equal widths.

Have fun with this! Come up with interesting combinations of strip widths for a nice variety of finished blocks. This is a great way to use leftover strips from other projects!

ARRANGING THE BLOCKS

1. Use a design wall or bed to place the blocks in five vertical rows, staggering the blocks. Don't worry about the triangles at this point. Extra triangles will be removed later. Rearrange the blocks until you are pleased with the arrangement. Rows One, Three, and Five each have seven blocks, and Rows Two and Four each have six blocks.

2. Refer to "Arranging the Blocks" on page 23 to create the design as shown in the Quilt Layout on the opposite page. Add and remove triangles as needed.

3. You will also need to fill in rows two and four with half blocks or background fabric as in the quilt in the photo. Use a completed block to make a template for cutting a half block, or see "Making Half Blocks" on page 22.

ASSEMBLING THE ROWS

Refer to "Assembling the Rows" on page 23 to sew the block units into rows.

BORDERS

This quilt has 2" finished background borders on the sides only. There is a wedge-pieced border around all four sides. You will need to turn the corner with a wedge piece, and the corners of the quilt are angled.

1. Measure the length of the quilt through the center. Piece the 2½" x 42" strips of the background

Shortcut from Blanche

Select a fabric with stripes, and cut it like a strip set to get the look of a strip-pieced block without piecing the strips!

fabric together and trim to the length needed. Make two border strips and sew them to the quilt sides.

2. Sew the B patches together using a ¼" seam allowance; begin sewing at the wide end, and stitch to the narrow end. You can sew the patches together randomly or lay them out in a planned arrangement. The top and bottom border strips consist of 34 patches each. The side borders consist of 51 each. There will be 4 patches left for the corners. Make sure that each border strip ends at the corner with a wedge that has the narrow end closest to the quilt.

Narrow ends

Narrow ends are next to quilt at the corners.

3. Sew the border units to the quilt, stopping about 2" from the corners.

4. Stitch another wedge with the wide end away from the quilt, to the end of the border. Then stitch it to the wedge that begins the adjacent border. This will make the border turn around the corner.

Corner wedge

Add the corner wedge.

5. Lay the quilt flat to determine if you need to take a deeper seam allowance on the corner wedge. Begin at the outer edge of the pieced border and stitch toward the inner edge, slightly increasing the seam allowance until you have sewn an additional ¼" on each side. This should create a pointed corner wedge on the right side of the border.

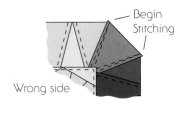

Begin Stitching

Wrong side

Right side

Stitch a deeper seam allowance on the corner wedge.

6. Finish stitching the wedge pieced border to the quilt. You will need to clip the seam allowance of the corner wedge piece so it aligns with both sides of the quilt.

Quilt Layout

Quilting

Strip Heaven was machine quilted with a somewhat wild continuous line design that zigzags here and there in a circular pattern. It was done in a variegated thread.

Binding

Refer to "Binding" on page 29 to bind the quilt.

Gallery Quilt

Midnight Jewel 2002

45" x 50"

Medium blocks; pieced and machine quilted by Blanche Young.

This wall hanging could be hung with the diamond setting going either horizontally or vertically. It features an uneven border cut in a wonderfully unique shape with a striped piping around the blocks and as the binding.

Quilt Layouts

Y ou can photocopy the quilt layouts on these pages to help plan and design your own Dresden Flower Garden quilt. Enlarge them, if desired, and use colored pencils to decide colors. Rotate the photocopies, add more blocks, use fewer blocks, add rows, or include half blocks as desired. Also use your photocopy to plan borders, either plain or pieced.

Basic Quilt Layout

Star Variation Layout

*Diamond
Variation Layout*

Large A

Small A

Large B

Small B

Note: ³⁄₈" seam allowance added for appliqué

Note: ½" allowed on inner edges of A and B templates for appliquéing center circle

Template Patterns

Medium C
(Cut Size)

Medium A

Medium B

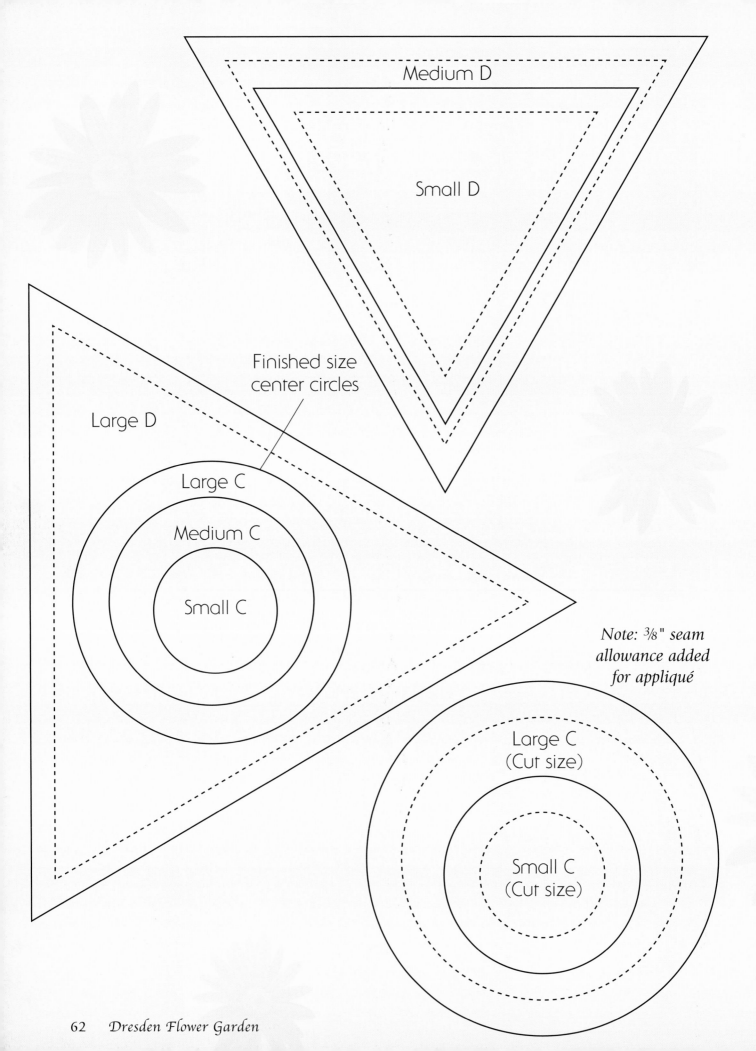

Medium D

Small D

Finished size
center circles

Large D

Large C

Medium C

Small C

Note: ⅜" seam
allowance added
for appliqué

Large C
(Cut size)

Small C
(Cut size)

About the Authors

BLANCHE YOUNG

Blanche Young is a familiar name and face in the world of quilting. She has had a life-long romance with fabric and sewing machines. Blanche has been teaching quiltmaking since 1970, after having worked for a dress factory and major sewing machine companies. By applying time-saving cutting, sewing, and construction techniques to her quiltmaking, she developed innovative methods that have made complex pieced patterns quicker and easier. Blanche is the author or co-author of ten books and many patterns.

Over the years, Blanche has taught and lectured all across the United States and in Japan and Norway. She has been the Featured Artist at numerous quilt shows. In October 2001, at Quilt Festival in Houston, Texas, she and her daughter Helen Young Frost were two of the six women chosen for a Special Exhibit entitled: "Women Who Challenged Quilting." Blanche is a true pioneer in quilting.

A prolific quiltmaker, Blanche makes several dozen quilts each year. She has donated more than sixty quilts for fundraising purposes to quilt guilds and groups across the country.

Blanche moved from California to Hurricane, Utah, in 2001. She has seven grown children, two dozen grandchildren and eight great-grandchildren.

LYNETTE YOUNG BINGHAM

Lynette Young Bingham has been involved in quilting, since the early 1970s when she and her sister Helen would drive into the Watts area of Los Angeles to purchase quilt batting by the pound to sell to Blanche's students. In 1979, Blanche, Helen, and Lynette formed Young Publications and self-published their first six books. Lynette handled the sales and distribution of the books, and represented the company at Quilt Market/Quilt Festival and other shows and conventions.

Lynette and her family live in Hurricane, Utah. Even though she is employed full-time as an Escrow Officer at a title company in St. George, Utah, she finds time to teach quilting classes locally. She owns several wonderful antique quilts and toy sewing machines and has an extensive Raggedy Ann and Andy collection.

Lynette and her husband, Jim, are the parents of one son and three daughters. They have four grandsons and four granddaughters, all age five and under, who all live within five miles of Papa and Grandma!

Resources

Brooklyn Revolver
Come Quilt with Me, Inc.
3903 Avenue I
Brooklyn, NY 11210
718-377-3652
email: Comequiltwithme@aol.com

Acrylic Templates for Dresden Flower Garden
Quilt Station
4210 E. Los Angeles Avenue
Simi Valley, CA 93063
805-584-6915
www.quiltstation.com

Quilting Supplies
Cotton Patch Mail Order
3405 Hall Lane, dept. CTB
Layayette, CA 94549
800-835-4418
925-283-7883
website: www.quiltusa.com
email: quiltusa@yahoo.com

Note: Fabrics used in the quilts shown may not be currently available since fabric manufacturers keep most fabrics in print for only a short time.

You can reach Blanche at:
455 South 400 West,
Hurricane, UT 84737
email: lynettebingham@aol.com

You can reach Lynette at:
51 West 810 South,
Hurricane, UT 84737
email: lynettebingham@aol.com

Also by Blanche Young and Dalene Young Stone:
Tradition with a Twist

For more information write for a free catalog:

C&T Publishing, Inc.
P.O. Box 1456
Lafayette, CA 94549
(800) 284-1114
e-mail: ctinfo@ctpub.com
website: www.ctpub.com

Index